Underwater Life: the Oceans

Words by Dean Morris

Raintree Childrens Books
Milwaukee • Toronto • Melbourne

Library of Congress Number: 77-23051

3 4 5 6 7 8 9 0 81 80 79

Printed and bound in the United States of América.

Library of Congress Cataloging in Publication Data

Morris, Dean.
  Underwater life: the oceans.

  (Read about)
  Includes index.
  SUMMARY: Describes plant and animal life in the ocean
and man's attempts to develop technology for deep
sea exploration.
  1. Marine biology— Juvenile literature.
[1. Marine biology. 2. Ocean bottom] I. Title.
QH91.16.M66   574.92   77-23051
ISBN 0-8393-0009-3

This book has been reviewed
for accuracy by

Dr. David H. Stansbery
Director and Professor
The Ohio State Museum of Zoology

Noel T. Wood
Captain, United States Navy
Professor of Naval Science
Marquette University

Underwater Life:
the Oceans

Most of the earth is covered by oceans. This picture shows how the part of the earth under the ocean looks.

The ocean floor is much like the land area of the earth. Some of it is sandy. Some of it is rocky. In some places it is muddy and soft. There are flat places called plains. There are deep cracks called chasms. There are high mountains and deep valleys.

Many underwater mountains are higher than those on land. Sometimes the tops of these underwater mountains stick up out

land

chasm

of the water. Then the mountain tops
are called islands. The chasms in the
floor of the sea may be very deep. If
the highest mountain on earth could be
dropped into the deepest chasm, it would not
show above the water.

The sea is always moving. Water moves
toward the shores and back. This kind
of movement is called tide. Waves move
in the same way. Another movement of
ocean water is called a current. A current
is like a large river that follows a course
through the sea.

island

land

mountain

plain

Tiny animals and plants, called plankton, live suspended in the sea. Some of them are too small to be seen except through a microscope.

This picture shows some kinds of plankton. They look much larger than they really are. You can see that they have many different shapes.

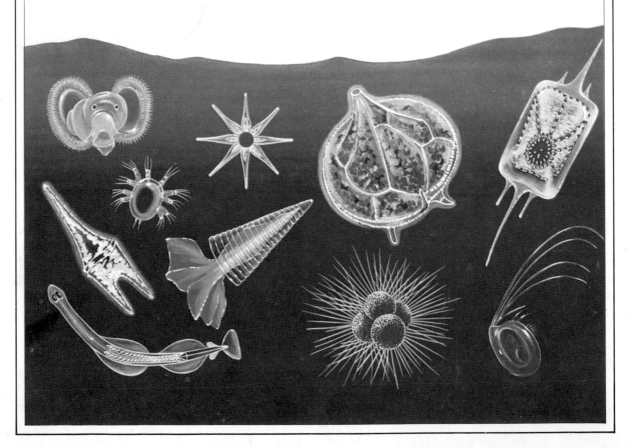

Like green plants on land, plankton
plants use sunlight to make their own food.
They are found near the top of the water
where there is plenty of sunlight. Plankton
animals eat the plankton plants. They
are found near the top of the sea too. Some
fish feed on the plankton plants and animals.

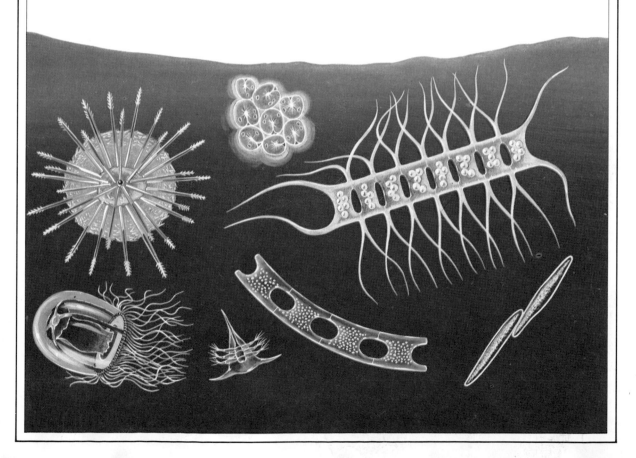

Whales are mammals, not fish. They live in the sea, but they breathe air. They have warm blood, hair, and mammary glands. Young whales are born live.

The largest whale of all is the blue whale. It is larger than any land animal that ever lived.

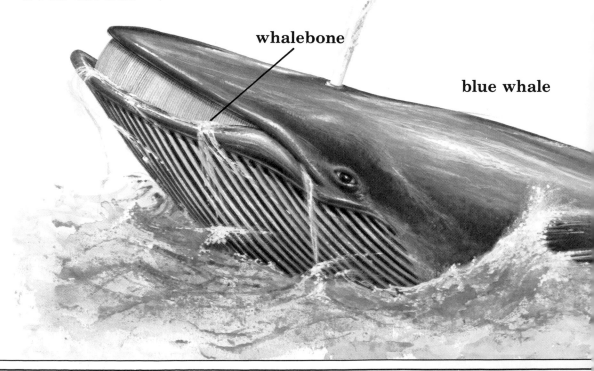

whalebone

blue whale

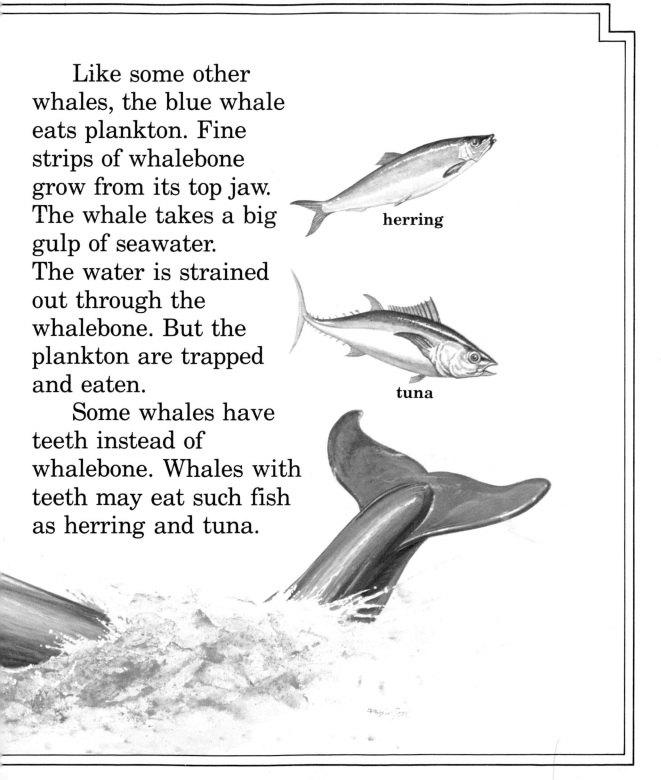

Like some other whales, the blue whale eats plankton. Fine strips of whalebone grow from its top jaw. The whale takes a big gulp of seawater. The water is strained out through the whalebone. But the plankton are trapped and eaten.

Some whales have teeth instead of whalebone. Whales with teeth may eat such fish as herring and tuna.

herring

tuna

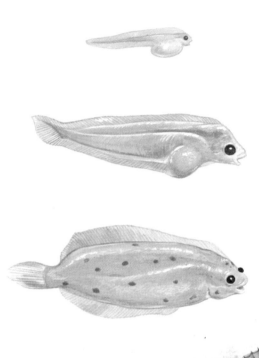

Flatfish are sea animals named for their shape. A young flatfish looks like other young fish. As it grows, its body becomes wide and flat. Its eyes change position. Both eyes are on the top side of the adult's body.

These pictures show how a plaice changes as it grows.

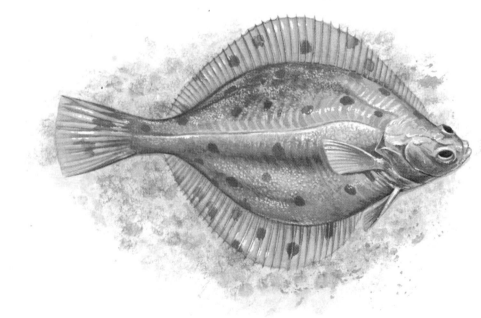

Flatfish like the plaice, the sole, and the skate lie on the seafloor.

The plaice lies on its left side. The top of the plaice's body is really its right side. Its skin is the color of the seabed.

A plaice may change color and often it looks like the color of the place it is lying. This plaice has black patches which match the checkerboard below it.

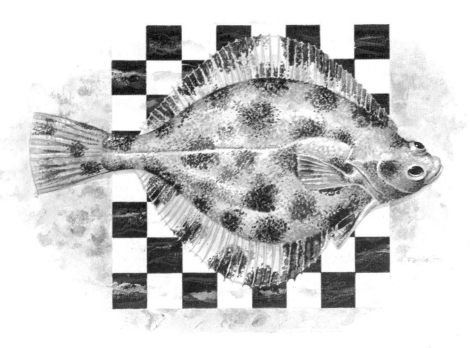

Many plants and animals live on the sea-floor. Many crabs and starfish live on the bottom near shore. Crabs can be seen on the beach, usually when the tide is out. Crabs have eight walking legs and two claws. On land, they often move by walking sideways. Most starfish have five arms that reach out from the middle of their bodies. Some have more arms. Starfish often eat shellfish.

Rays have flat bodies. They swim smoothly through the sea as if they were flying.

ray

starfish

crab

The octopus has eight long arms. They are called tentacles.

The octopus eats other sea animals. It catches and holds them with its tentacles.

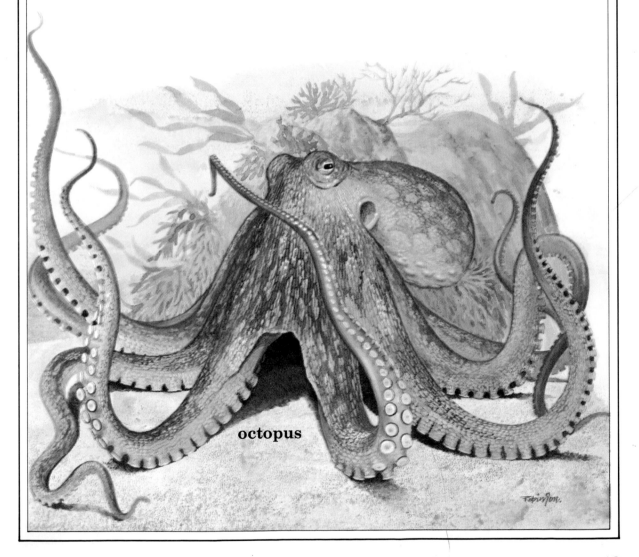

octopus

People dive underwater for sponges. A sponge is a kind of sea animal. Some can soak up water and stay wet for a long time.

People use sponge skeletons as washcloths or scrubbing cloths.

This diver collects living sponges in a net bag. He stays under the water until he needs another breath of air.

sponges

The oyster is a sea animal called a mollusk. It lives on the seabed. It does not swim.

Some people like to eat oysters. Oysters are often grown for food on special ocean farms.

Oysters cover the inside of their shells with a lining. The lining of some oysters is called mother-of-pearl. It is smooth and shiny. Sometimes a piece of grit gets into a pearl oyster's shell. The pearl oyster covers the grit with mother-of-pearl. It becomes a gem called a pearl. Some pearls are worth a lot of money.

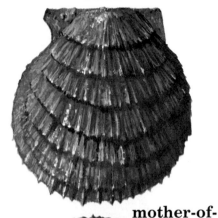

oyster shell

mother-of-pearl

pearl

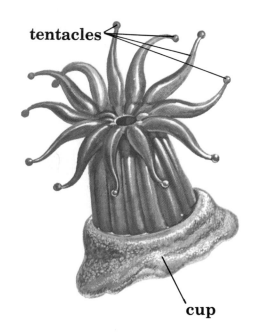

coral animal

tentacles

cup

Corals are small sea animals. They have hollow, round bodies. The coral secretes a cup around itself. The cup is like stone. One end of the coral's body fits into the cup. At the other end are tentacles used to catch food.

Corals live in large groups. They grow close together.

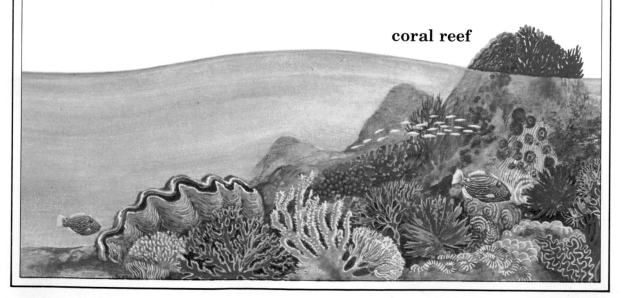

coral reef

When coral animals die, new cups are built on and around the old ones. After a while a wall of coral cups is formed. The wall is called a reef.

Coral reefs are found in warm parts of the world. Some islands have coral reefs built up all the way around them.

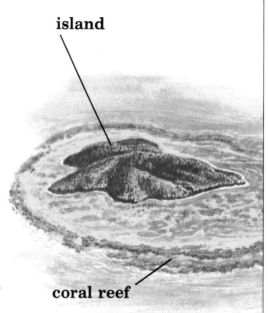

island

coral reef

In the deepest parts of the ocean it is cold and dark. The light and heat from the sun do not reach the water there. Fish that live in deep water do not look like the fish that live in shallow water.

Some deep-water fish are able to make their own light. Some have lights along their sides. Others carry lights like lanterns on their heads. Some deep-sea fish have large eyes. They help the fish see the lights of other fish.

The gulper eel is a deep-sea fish with a very large mouth. It can swallow a sea animal that is wider than its own body.

When sea animals and plants die, they sink to the bottom. Deep-sea fish eat them. They eat one another too.

19

People eat many kinds of fish. Cod, herring, tuna, and flounder are some of the food fish. Fishermen know many ways to catch different kinds of fish.

Herring swim near the top of the sea. Fishermen use drift nets to catch them. This picture shows a fishing boat with a drift net. The net has floats to keep it up near the top of the sea. The herring swim into the net. They cannot get out.

drifter

floats

drift net

Cod live near the bottom of the sea. A trawl net is used to catch fish that swim near the bottom.

A fishing boat called a trawler drags a net through the water. Fish are caught in the net. When the net is full of fish, it is pulled in. The fish make the net very heavy. A machine called a winch helps drag the net back.

Trawlers carry ice to keep the fish cold. The fish need to be kept fresh all the way back to the port.

trawler

trawl net

These divers are exploring the seabed.
They wear masks over their noses and eyes.
The clear covering helps them see.
They carry air in tanks on their backs.
They breathe air through tubes.

The divers wear rubber flippers on their feet. The flippers help them move faster when they want to swim after a fish. They are using a waterproof camera to film a shark.

Deep-sea divers wear special clothes.
Their suits keep them warm while they are
in the cold water. Weights make them heavy
so they can stay on the seabed. Air hoses
fit into their helmets. Air is pumped to
the divers from above the water.

These divers are exploring the remains of a ship. The ship sank a long time ago. Not much of it is left. The divers have found a cannon. The cannon is going to be lifted up out of the water. Then the divers will look for other things.

These divers are working underwater.
They are fixing holes in a ship that sank.
They use tools to put metal patches over
the holes. The divers use strong lights
to see what they are doing.

When the holes are fixed, no more water
can get in. Doors and other openings
will be closed tight. Air will be pumped
into the ship. The water that is inside
the ship will be pumped out. Then the
ship will float up to the top of the sea.

Submarines are ships that can go underwater as well as on top of the sea.

A submarine has tanks at each side of its hull. They are called ballast tanks. They are open to the sea at the bottom and have large valves on top. When the submarine is on the surface, the ballast tanks are full of air. To submerge, the large valves are opened to let the air out. As the air goes out, the water comes in and the submarine goes under the water.

Nautilus

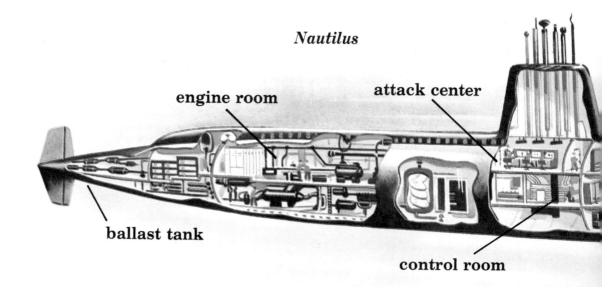

engine room

attack center

ballast tank

control room

Air is blown into the ballast tanks to make the submarine come up. The air forces water out.

The *Nautilus* uses atomic energy. Its engines do not need air to work. Submarines that use atomic energy can stay underwater longer than ordinary submarines.

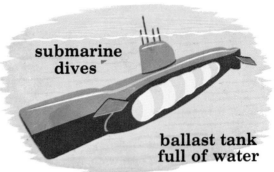

submarine
dives

ballast tank
full of water

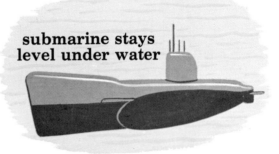

submarine stays
level under water

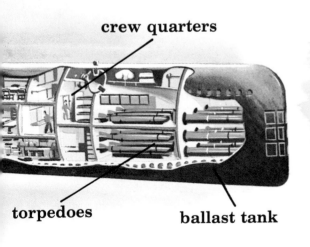

crew quarters

torpedoes

ballast tank

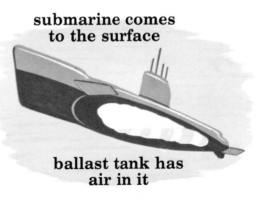

submarine comes
to the surface

ballast tank has
air in it

Other ships can go underwater too. The
bathyscaphe is used to go to the deepest
parts of the sea. The bathyscaphe in the
picture is the *Trieste I*. When it was
built in 1953, it could go deeper than any
other ship.

ballast tanks

cabin

Bathyscaphes have a cabin underneath. It is shaped like a ball. The crew is in the cabin. They can look through the windows. They can see deep-sea animals and take underwater pictures.

light

We get many useful things from the sea. Oil, coal, gas, and valuable minerals can all be found under the seafloor.

People eat fish. Fish are used to help plants grow better too. Some people use seaweed as a food. We know that sea plants can be used for other things too. People are trying to find new ways to use them. They may be more valuable to people if they are left in the sea.

Salt in seawater can be taken out of the water. Then the water can be used to grow plants in dry places. However, this costs a great deal of money.

Someday people may work and live under the sea. They may raise fish on farms. They may grow crops of underwater plants. People may use submarines to travel underwater. They will have to live in watertight houses. These people will be able to make their fresh air from the water around them.

submarines

houses

bathyscaphe

Where to Read About the Underwater Life

Pronunciation Key for Glossary

a	a as in **cat**, **bad**
ā	a as in **able**, ai as in **train**, ay as in **play**
ä	a as in **father**, **car**
e	e as in **bend**, **yet**
ē	e as in **me**, ee as in **feel**, ea as in **beat**, ie as in **piece**, y as in **heavy**
i	i as in **in**, **pig**
ī	i as in **ice**, **time**, ie as in **tie**, y as in **my**
o	o as in **top**
ō	o as in **old**, oa as in **goat**, ow as in **slow**, oe as in **toe**
ô	o as in **cloth**, au as in **caught**, aw as in **paw**, a as in **all**
oo	oo as in **good**, u as in **put**
o͞o	oo as in **tool**, ue as in **blue**
oi	oi as in **oil**, oy as in **toy**
ou	ou as in **out**, ow as in **plow**
u	u as in **up**, **gun**, o as in **other**
ur	ur as in **fur**, er as in **person**, ir as in **bird**, or as in **work**
yo͞o	u as in **use**, ew as in **few**
ə	a as in **again**, e as in **broken**, i as in **pencil**, o as in **attention**, u as in **surprise**
ch	ch as in **such**
ng	ng as in **sing**
sh	sh as in **shell**, **wish**
th	th as in **three**, **bath**
<u>th</u>	th as in **that**, **together**

GLOSSARY

These words are defined the way they are used in this book.

adult (ə dult' *or* ad' ult) a person, animal, or plant that is grown up; mature

area (er' ē ə) a certain place or part of the world

atomic energy (ə tom' ik en' ər jē) energy released from the nucleus of an atom, used to make electricity to run machines

ballast tank (bal' əst tangk) a compartment on a submarine that is filled with air when the submarine floats and with water when it submerges

bathyscaphe (bath' i skaf' *or* bath' i skāf') a vessel used to explore places under the sea

beach (bēch) gently sloping land at the edge of an ocean or lake

blood (blud) a red liquid pumped from the heart through veins and arteries to all parts of the body

blown (blōn) moved with force

body (bod′ ē) the whole of a person, animal, or plant

breathe (brēth) to take air into the lungs and then force it out

built (bilt) made by putting a number of things together

camera (kam′ ər ə *or* kam′ rə) a device used to take photographs

cannon (kan′ ən) a large, heavy gun that is mounted on a base or on wheels

cannot (kan′ ot *or* ka not′) is not able; can not

chasm (kaz′ əm) a deep crack or opening in the surface of the earth

checkerboard (chek′ ər bôrd′) a square board that is marked off in alternating squares of two different colors

claw (klô) a sharp, curved nail on an animal's foot

coal (kōl) a black substance found under the ground which is used by man

collect (kə lekt′) to bring several things together

cost (kôst) to be bought at a certain price

crew (krōō) a group of people who work together to make a train, ship, or plane run

crop (krop) plants that are grown for something useful such as food

current (kur′ ənt) part of a body of water that moves along in a certain path or course

dive (dīv) to go down under the water

diver (dī′ vər) a person who explores places underwater

drag (drag) to pull something along slowly

drift net (drift net) a fishing net that is moved slowly by water currents and wind

eaten (ēt′ ən) taken in through the mouth and swallowed

engine (en′ jin) a machine that uses energy to run another machine

explore (eks plôr′) to travel or to examine unknown places to learn what they are like

film (film) to take pictures with a camera

fishermen (fish′ ər mən) people who fish to get food or for the fun of fishing

fix (fiks) to make something work or to put something together after it breaks

flipper (flip′ ər) a rubber foot covering worn by swimmers and divers to help them move faster

float (flōt) to rest on top of air or water or to move slowly through air or water; an object that floats

force (fôrs) to cause something to happen by using great strength

form (fôrm) to make or shape

gas (gas) matter that is not liquid or solid and has no shape

gem (jem) a mineral or pearl that has value because it is not common

great deal (grāt dēl) large amount

grit (grit) a tiny piece of sand or stone

grown (grōn) raised to produce a crop

heat (hēt) warmth; the state of being hot; to make warm or hot

helmet (hel′ mit) a head cover that is used to keep a person from being hurt

hose (hōz) a tube that can be bent easily,

used to carry air or liquid from one place
to another

hull (hul) a ship's sides and bottom

island (ī′ lənd) a piece of land with water on
all sides of it

jaw (jô) the top or bottom hard mouthpart of a
person or animal

lantern (lan′ tərn) a light with a covering,
usually able to be carried

mammal (mam′ əl) a warm-blooded animal
with mammary glands and hair

mammary gland (mam′ ə rē gland) a gland
found in mammals which may produce milk

mask (mask) an eye or face covering used to
hide or protect

metal (met′ əl) a shiny kind of material that
can be melted and made into shapes for tools
and other things that need to be strong

microscope (mī′ krə skōp′) a device used to
look at very small things through a lens that
makes them look larger

mineral (min′ ər əl) a material found in earth,
water, or air which has never been alive

mollusk (mol′ əsk) an animal that has a mantle that usually secretes a shell

movement (mo͞ov′ mənt) changing the place or direction of something

net (net) loose material made of threads or cord knotted together so that there are many holes; used to catch fishes, insects, or other animals

oil (oil) a greasy substance that does not mix with water

ordinary (ôrd′ ən er′ ē) usual; common; not different from others

patch (pach) a small piece of material used to cover a hole or repair something

pearl (purl) a hard body formed inside some mollusks

port (pôrt) a waterfront city with a place where ships can come and go

position (pə zish′ ən) the place where something or someone is

pump (pump) to move a liquid from one place to another with a machine

reef (rēf) a ridge of rock or coral that is found at or near the surface of a body of water

remains (ri mānz′) all that is left of something; a dead body

rubber (rub′ ər) a strong, stretchable material made from the liquid of certain plants

sank (sangk) went down or through something such as water

scrub (skrub) to rub hard in order to clean something

seabed (sē′ bed′) the land that is under the sea

seafloor (sē′ flôr) the floor of the ocean

secrete (si krēt′) to form and give off a substance

shallow (shal′ ō) not deep

shellfish (shel′ fish′) an animal that lives in water and has a shell

sideways (sīd′ wāz′) a movement to or from the side

sink (singk) to go down or through something such as water

skeleton (skel′ ə tən) a firm frame of bones or shell in or around the body of a person or animal

skin (skin) the outer covering of a person's or some animals' bodies

smooth (smo͞oth) not rough; even or level

smoothly (smo͞oth' lē) in a way that is not rough or uneven; gracefully

soak (sōk) to make very wet; to take in a great deal of a liquid and hold it

someday (sum' dā') at some time in the future

strained (strānd) poured through a material that lets smaller things, but not larger solids, pass

strip (strip) a long, narrow piece of a material

submarine (sub' mə rēn') a ship that can move about on the surface or underwater

submerge (səb murj') to go underneath a body of water

sunlight (sun' līt') the light that comes from the sun

suspended (sə spend' id) held in place

swallow (swol' ō) to take food in through the mouth and into the gut

taken (tā' kən) removed from

tank (tangk) a large container used to

hold a liquid or a gas

tentacle (ten′ tə kəl) an armlike growth of a sea animal used to touch, grasp, or help the animal move

tide (tīd) the movement of oceans and other large bodies of water that causes a rise and fall about every twelve hours

tool (to͞ol) something a person uses to do work or to make something

travel (trav′ əl) to move from one place to another

trawl net (trôl net) a net on a long line that is dragged slowly along the seabed to catch fish

trawler (trôl′ ər) a boat used for fishing along the seabed

tube (to͞ob *or* tyo͞ob) a hollow piece of material shaped like a pipe

underneath (un′ dər nēth′) below or under something

underwater (un′ dər wô′ tər) below the surface of a body of water

useful (yo͞os′ fəl) helpful; able to serve a purpose

valuable (val′ y$\overline{oo}$ ə bəl *or* val yə bəl) having great value; worth a great deal

valve (valv) a device that is turned to open or close a pipe or tube through which liquids flow

waterproof (wo′ tər pr$\overline{oo}$f′) able to keep water from passing through

watertight (wo′ tər t$\overline{i}$t′) made waterproof; see **waterproof**

weight (w$\overline{a}$t) something heavy that is used to hold down a person or thing

whalebone (hw$\overline{a}$l′ b$\overline{o}$n′) a horny substance that grows on the jaws of a whale

winch (winch) a machine used to lift or pull something heavy

Bibliography

Burton, Maurice, and Burton, Robert, editors.
   The International Wildlife Encyclopedia.
   20 vols. Milwaukee: Purnell Reference
   Books, 1970.

Eckert, Allan W. *In Search of a Whale.*
   Garden City, N.Y.: Doubleday & Company, 1970.
   Describes the difficulties and animals
   encountered by the crew of the *Geronimo*
   on their voyage to capture a whale, the
   most difficult animal to bring back
   alive.

Fisher, James. *The Wonderful World of the
   Sea.* Garden City, N.Y.: Doubleday & Company,
   1970.
   Tells the story of the sea and man's
   relationship to it from the appearance of
   the first living things in the ocean to the
   development of modern scientific navigation
   and underwater exploration.

Jacobs, Francine. *Sea Turtles.* New York:
   William Morrow & Company, 1972.
   Discusses the physical characteristics,
   habits, and habitats of the five species
   of sea turtles.

McClung, Robert M. *Treasures in the Sea.*
   Washington, D.C.: National Geographic
   Society, 1972.
   Describes some of the treasures to be
   found in the seas, including cargoes
   from wrecked ships, valuable shells,
   and pearls.